HELLO BUFFALO!

BY MARK CLOUD

CHACHABACHA
BOOKS

For Mary Jane and Anna Kathryn -
my Buffalo gals.

Buffalo, New York. It's an amazing place.
It's got all kinds of wonderful things.

Things like…

Astounding architecture.

Grand old homes.

And a lighthouse.

A place for saving presidencies.

And a place for
saving money.

Botanical gardens.

A science museum.

ROTHKO

Oh, and art museums. Incredible art museums.

Iconic high-rises.

A zoo.

TED'S
7
ARTIN
VIVA LOS BILLS
VIVA LOS BILLS
VIVA LOS BILLS
VIVA LOS BILLS

NORTH PARK
NORTH PARK
HAPPY DYNGUS DAY!
NP
LETS GO BUFFALO!
AN EVENING WITH
Ella FITZGERALD
JAZZ
APRIL 30 - 8:15 p.m.
THE SUPREMES
SUN. DEC. 6
ONE NIGHT ONLY
TWO SHOWS

Fantastic theaters.

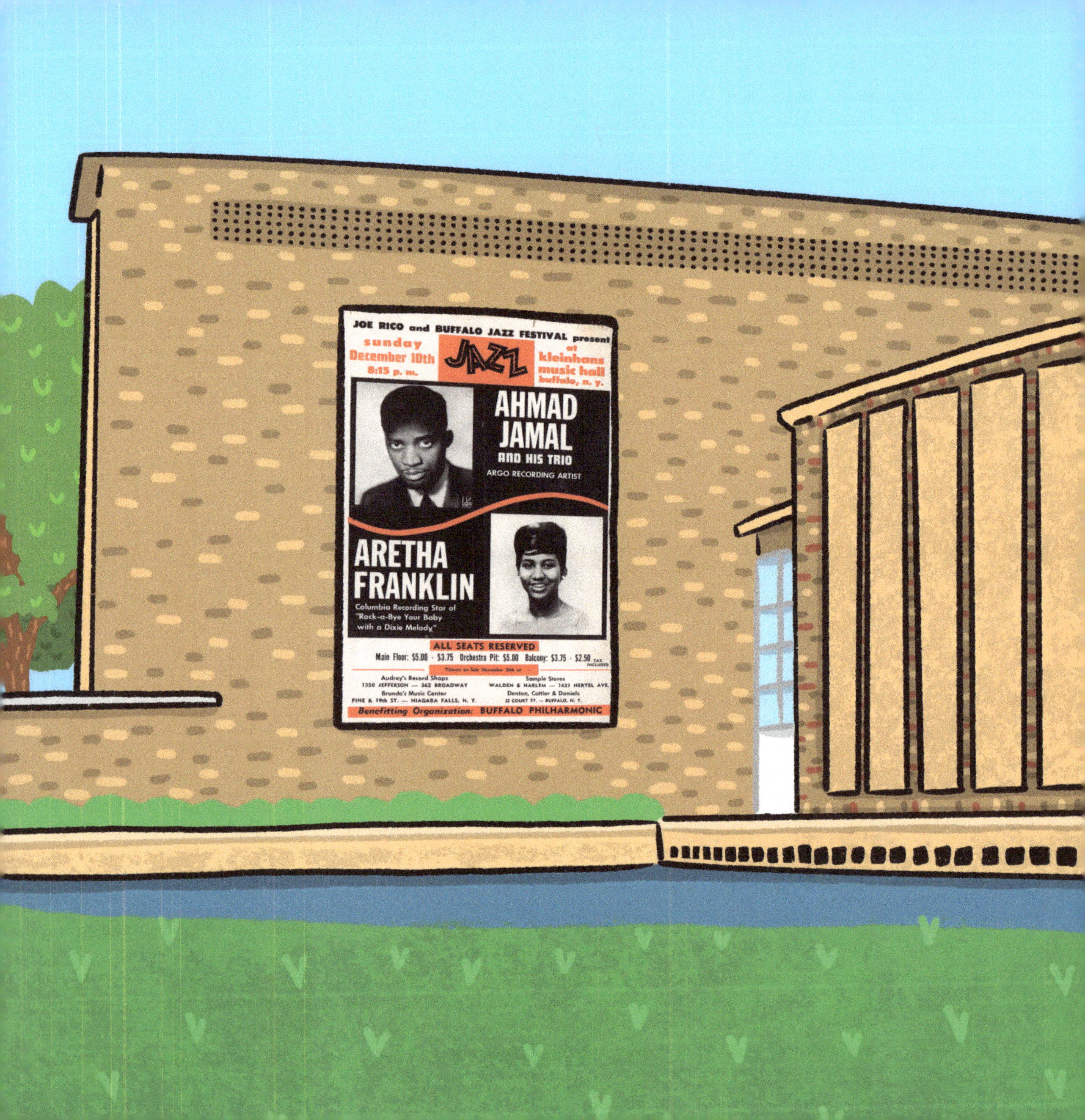
JOE RICO and BUFFALO JAZZ FESTIVAL present
sunday
December 10th
8:15 p.m.
JAZZ
at
kleinhans
music hall
buffalo, n. y.
AHMAD
JAMAL
AND HIS TRIO
ARGO RECORDING ARTIST
ARETHA
FRANKLIN
Columbia Recording Star of
"Rock-a-Bye Your Baby
with a Dixie Melody"
ALL SEATS RESERVED
Main Floor: $5.00 - $3.75 Orchestra Pit: $5.00 Balcony: $3.75 - $2.50 TAX INCLUDED
Audrey's Record Shops
1350 JEFFERSON — 362 BROADWAY
Brundo's Music Center
PINE & 19th ST. — NIAGARA FALLS, N. Y.
Sample Stores
WALDEN & HARLEM — 1631 HERTEL AVE.
Denton, Cottier & Daniels
32 COURT ST. — BUFFALO, N. Y.
Benefitting Organization: BUFFALO PHILHARMONIC

Places for music. Lots of them, actually.

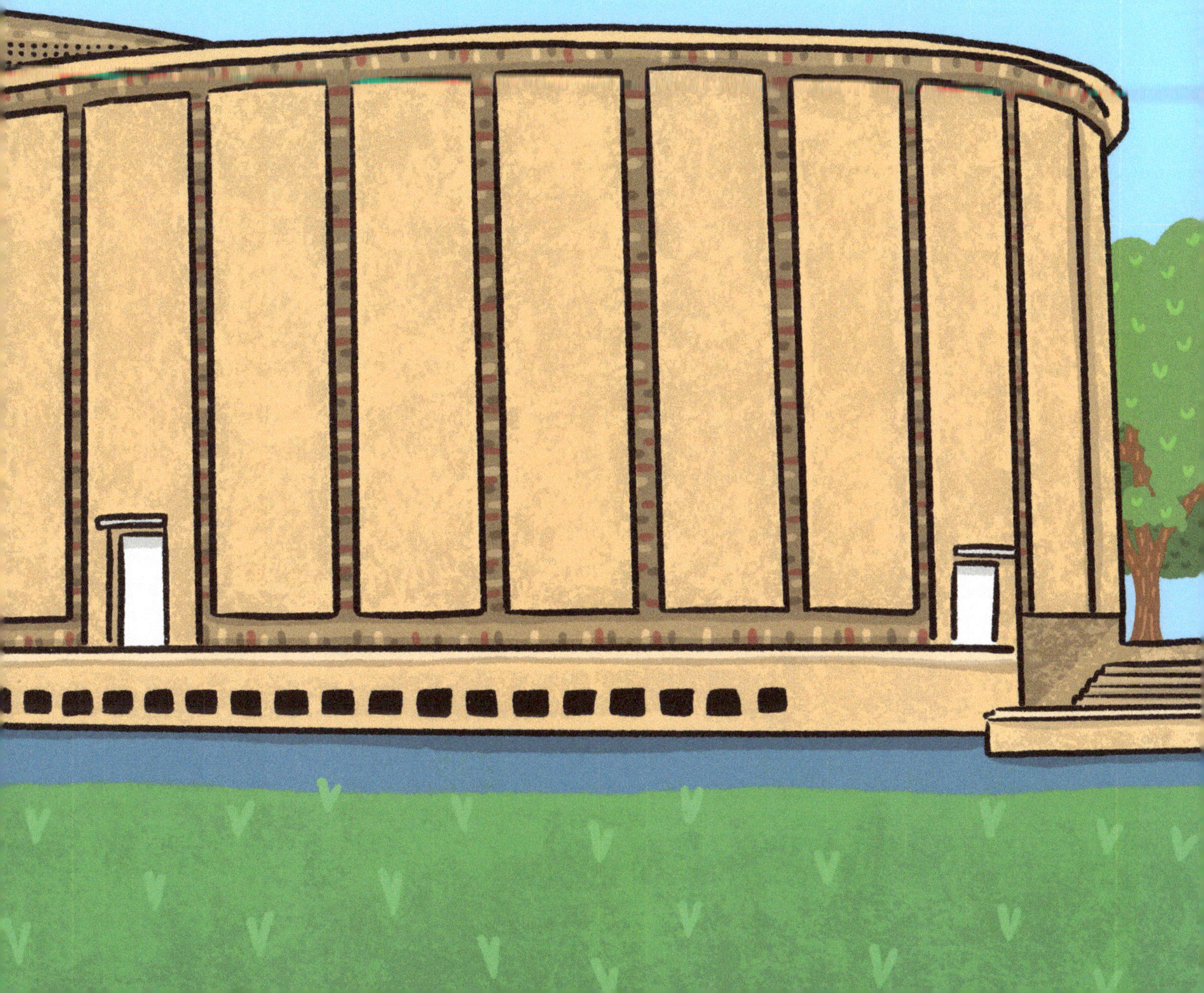

Fancy hotels.

Statues of liberty -
yes, two of them.

Beat *that* Big Apple!

The birthplace of buffalo wings.

And sports - with some of the greatest sports fans on the planet, win or lose. Or lose.

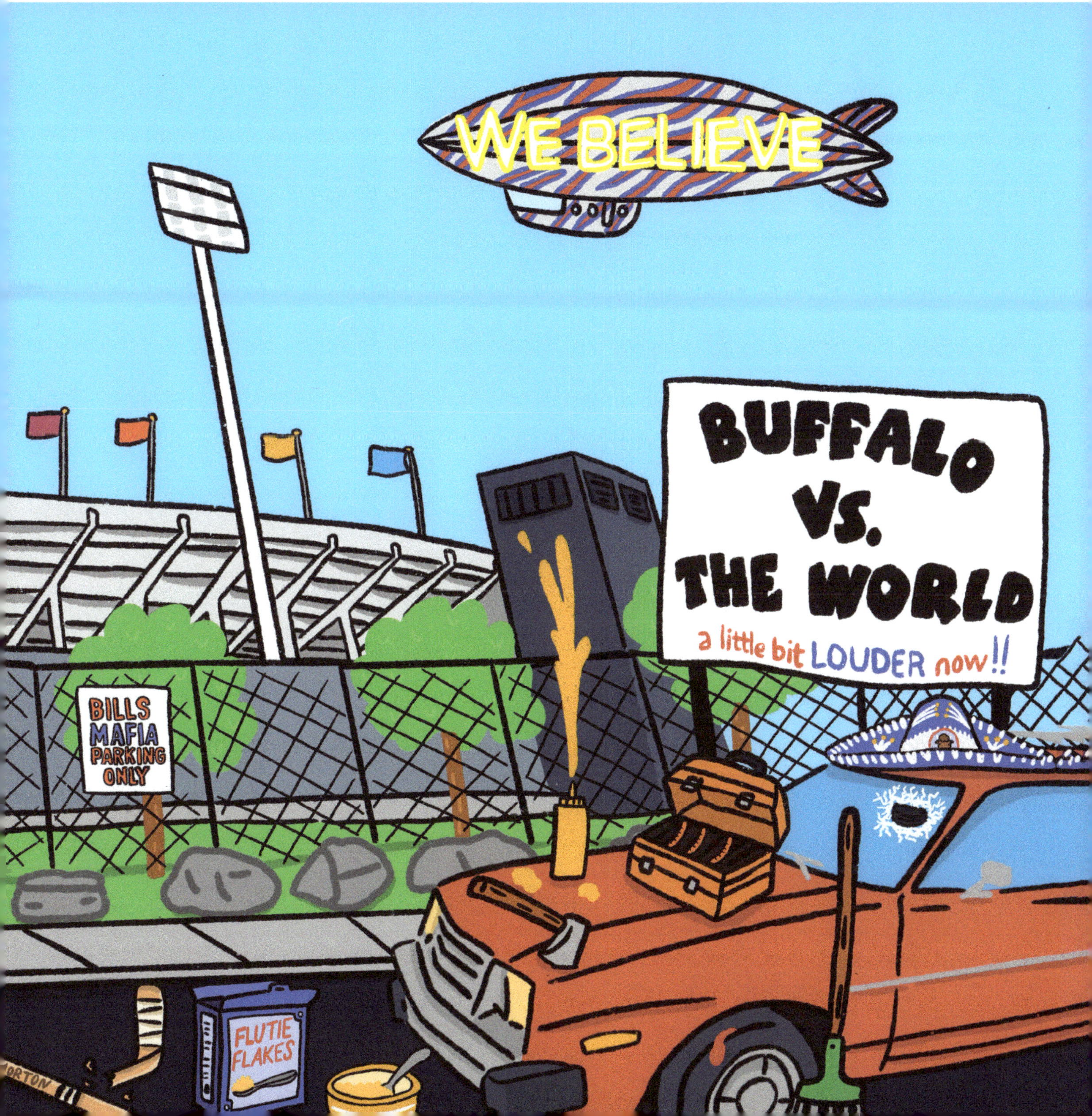
WE BELIEVE
BUFFALO VS. THE WORLD
a little bit LOUDER now!!
BILLS MAFIA PARKING ONLY
FLUTIE FLAKES

See? Buffalo is a wonderful place. Now, go tell your friends.

www.ingramcontent.com/pod-product-compliance
Ingram Content Group UK Ltd.
Pitfield, Milton Keynes, MK11 3LW, UK
UKHW060119010826
14089UKWH00005B/59

9 798868 942358